.50

About Raptors

For the One who created raptors.

—Genesis 1:20

Published by
PEACHTREE PUBLISHERS
1700 Chattahoochee Avenue
Atlanta, Georgia 30318-2112
www.peachtree-online.com

Text © 2010 by Cathryn P. Sill
Illustrations © 2010 by John C. Sill

Illustrations created in watercolor on archival quality 100% rag watercolor paper
Text and titles set in Novarese from Adobe Systems

Printed in May 2010 by Imago in Singapore
10 9 8 7 6 5 4 3 2 1
First Edition

Library of Congress Cataloging-in-Publication Data

Sill, Cathryn P., 1953-
 About raptors / written by Cathryn Sill ; illustrated by John Sill.
  p. cm.
 ISBN 978-1-56145-536-2 / 1-56145-536-9
 1. Birds of prey--Juvenile literature. I. Sill, John, ill. II. Title.
 QL677.78.S55 2010
 598.9--dc22
                    2009040348

About Raptors

A Guide for Children

Cathryn Sill

Illustrated by John Sill

Ω

PEACHTREE

ATLANTA

Raptors are birds of prey that hunt
and eat other animals.

They have hooked beaks for tearing meat
into bite-sized pieces.

PLATE 2
Bald Eagle

Most raptors have strong feet with sharp claws
that help them catch and hold prey.

PLATE 3
Red-tailed Hawk

Raptors search for prey by looking and listening.

PLATE 4
Secretary Bird

They fly and hunt in different ways.

a.

c.

b.

Some raptors capture prey in the air.

PLATE 6
Merlin
(*also shown: Violet-green Swallow*)

Others hunt for animals on the ground.

PLATE 7
Golden Eagle
(also shown: Black-tailed Jackrabbit)

Some raptors snatch food from the water.

PLATE 8
Osprey

Others hunt for animals that are already dead.

Raptors may hunt during the day…

or at night.

PLATE 11
Tawny Owl
(also shown: House Mouse)

Raptors use different kinds of nests to care for their babies.

Some raptors have large nests high in trees.

Others use holes to protect their eggs and chicks.

PLATE 14
Elf Owl

Some raptors have nests on cliffs or ledges.

PLATE 15
Prairie Falcon

Others nest on the ground.

PLATE 16
Short-eared Owl

Raptors live almost everywhere in the world.

a.

b.

c.

d.

e.

It is important to protect raptors and
the places where they live.

Afterword

PLATE 1

There are around 450 types of raptors in the world. The word "raptor" comes from the Latin word *rapere* that means "to seize" or "to snatch away." Raptors live on every continent except Antarctica. Great Gray Owls are one of the largest owls. They have a wingspan of up to 60 inches (152 cm). Great Gray Owls live in the northern parts of North America, Europe, and Asia.

PLATE 2

Raptors are predators whose diets include small mammals, fish, reptiles, amphibians, birds, and insects. A very few raptors sometimes eat fruit. Bald Eagles eat mostly fish. They live near large bodies of water across most of North America.

PLATE 3

The sharp claws on raptor's feet are called talons. When a raptor catches its prey, the talons lock into the animal and keep it from escaping. Red-tailed Hawks, the most common hawks in North America, are often seen perched on dead trees or utility poles along roadsides. They live throughout most of North America and parts of Central America.

PLATE 4

Raptors have large eyes and are able to see very well. They also have good hearing, which helps them find prey they cannot see. Secretary Birds hunt by walking along looking for food on the ground. They kill their prey by kicking it with their long legs and thick toes. Secretary Birds live in Africa.

PLATE 5

Raptors fly different ways according to the shape of their wings. Turkey Vultures have long broad wings and can soar for hours as they hunt in North, Central, and South America. Northern Goshawks have short, rounded wings so they can fly through forests while they hunt in North America, Europe, and Asia. Gyrfalcons have long, pointed wings and fly very fast as they chase prey in and near the Arctic.

PLATE 6

Falcons are fast, powerful flyers that can overtake prey in midair. Some falcons knock their prey to the ground. Others capture prey in the air. Merlins are small falcons that are able to catch flying songbirds. They live in North America and Eurasia.

PLATE 7

Some raptors hunt by sitting quietly on a perch waiting for prey to move. Others hunt as they soar in the air. After locating their prey, they swoop down and grab it. Golden Eagles are powerful hunters that use both of these hunting styles. They live in North America, Europe, Asia, and northern Africa.

PLATE 8

Most fishing raptors grab their prey just below the surface of the water. Ospreys sweep their wings back and dive in feetfirst. They have rough pads on their feet that help them hold the slippery fish. Ospreys live in many places all over the world.

PLATE 9

Some raptors are scavengers. Instead of looking for live prey, vultures hunt and eat carrion. Most vultures have nearly bare heads. The lack of feathers on their heads helps keep vultures clean and germ-free when they eat rotting meat. Vultures are very helpful as "nature's garbage collectors." Sometimes more than one kind of vulture will feed on the same dead animal. Rüppell's Griffons and African White-backed Vultures live in Africa.

PLATE 10

Diurnal raptors include hawks, eagles, falcons, vultures, and kites. Kites are graceful flyers that hunt during the day. Man-made kites got their name from these birds because of the way they hover in the air just as the birds do. Swallow-tailed Kites hunt by swooping and gliding over wet areas in the southeastern United States, Central America, and tropical South America.

PLATE 11

Most owls are nocturnal or crepuscular. A few hunt during the day. Owls can see very well in the dark. In total darkness they rely on their good hearing to locate prey. Soft feathers make their flight almost silent. This allows them to sneak up on the animals they eat. Tawny Owls are common in parts of Europe, northern Africa, and Asia.

PLATE 12

Some raptors use nests that have been built and abandoned by other birds, but most build their own nests. Northern Harriers make their nests on the ground with small sticks and grass. They often nest above the waterline in wet, marshy places. The father hunts for food while the mother stays at the nest to care for the eggs and chicks after they hatch. Northern Harriers live in North America, Europe, and Asia.

PLATE 13

Some raptors use branches, twigs, leaves, and grass to build nests in trees. Harpy Eagles build nests in the tallest trees in the rainforest. They are among the largest and most powerful raptors. Harpy Eagles have huge talons that help them catch larger mammals such as sloths and monkeys. They live in tropical forests from southeastern Mexico to South America.

PLATE 14

Raptors that nest in holes do not create them. They use holes made by other birds or animals. Elf Owls often nest in holes made by woodpeckers in giant cactuses or trees. Elf Owls, at 5 1/2 inches (14cm), are one of the smallest raptors in the world. They live in southwestern United States and Mexico.

PLATE 15

Some raptors that raise their chicks on cliffs and ledges do not build a nest. They scrape out a place in the dirt and gravel to lay their eggs. Prairie Falcons sometimes use an old nest made by another bird, but often they lay their eggs in a scraped place on a sheltered ledge. Prairie Falcons live in dry habitats in western North America.

PLATE 16

In some habitats, raptors nest on the ground because there are no suitable high places. Short-eared Owls live in open areas such as grasslands, marshes, and tundra. The mother owl builds a nest by scraping a place on the ground and lining it with grass and downy feathers. She may locate the nest near tall grass or shrubs for protection. Short-eared Owls live on every continent except Australia and Antarctica.

PLATE 17

Raptors are found in almost every habitat on Earth. Red-shouldered Hawks usually live near wet places in parts of North America. Snowy Owls live in tundra in the northern parts of Eurasia, North America, and the Arctic. Collared Forest Falcons live in tropical forests in Central and South America. Common Barn Owls often live in man-made structures in many places all over the world. Harris's Hawks live in deserts in parts of North, Central, and South America.

PLATE 18

Raptors are a valuable part of our world. They hunt rodents, insects, and other animals that destroy crops and damage property. Many kinds of raptors are in danger because of illegal hunting, pesticides, pollution, and habitat destruction. At one time Peregrine Falcons were nearly extinct in parts of the United States. Pesticides such as DDT made their eggshells thin and easily broken, causing the babies to die. Peregrine Falcon numbers are growing in places where DDT is no longer used. They live in many different habitats all over the world.

GLOSSARY

Carrion—dead and decaying flesh
Crepuscular—active at dawn and dusk
Diurnal—active during the day
Habitat—the place where animals and plants live
Nocturnal—active during the night
Predator—an animal that lives by hunting and eating other animals
Pesticide—chemical used to kill insects or other pests
Prey—animals that are hunted and eaten by other animals
Soar—to glide or fly in the air without flapping wings
Tropical—having to do with the area around the equator
Tundra—large treeless areas in arctic regions

BIBLIOGRAPHY

BOOKS

BIRDS OF PREY *by Wayne Lynch and Laura Evert (Northwood)*
BIRDS OF PREY OF THE WORLD *by Robin Chittenden (A Golden Guide from St. Martin's Press)*
EAGLE & BIRDS OF PREY *by Jemima Parry-Jones (Dorling Kindersley)*
RAPTOR! A KID'S GUIDE TO BIRDS OF PREY *by Christyna & René Laubach and Charles W. G. Smith (Storey Publishing)*
RAPTORS *by Bobbie Kalman (Crabtree Publishing Company)*

WEBSITES

http://www.carolinaraptorcenter.org/species.php
http://www.peregrinefund.org/explore_raptors/index.html
http://www.raptorchapter.org/HawkTalk.htm

Also in the ABOUT... series

ABOUT THE SILLS

Cathryn Sill, a former elementary school teacher, is the author of the acclaimed ABOUT... series as well as the ABOUT HABITATS series. With her husband John and brother-in-law Ben Sill, she coauthored three popular bird-guide parodies, including A FIELD GUIDE TO LITTLE-KNOWN AND SELDOM-SEEN BIRDS OF NORTH AMERICA.

John Sill is a prize-winning and widely published wildlife artist who illustrated both the ABOUT... series and the ABOUT HABITATS series, and illustrated and coauthored the FIELD GUIDES. A native of North Carolina, he holds a B.S. in Wildlife Biology from North Carolina State University.

The Sills live and work in Franklin, North Carolina.

Books in the ABOUT... and ABOUT HABITATS series

ISBN 978-1-56145-028-2 HC
ISBN 978-1-56145-147-0 PB

ISBN 978-1-56145-141-8 HC
ISBN 978-1-56145-174-6 PB

ISBN 978-1-56145-183-8 HC
ISBN 978-1-56145-233-0 PB

ISBN 978-1-56145-207-1 HC
ISBN 978-1-56145-232-3 PB

ISBN 978-1-56145-234-7 HC
ISBN 978-1-56145-312-2 PB

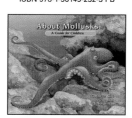
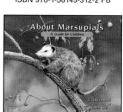

ISBN 978-1-56145-256-9 HC
ISBN 978-1-56145-335-1 PB

ISBN 978-1-56145-038-1 HC
ISBN 978-1-56145-364-1 PB

ISBN 978-1-56145-301-6 HC
ISBN 978-1-56145-405-1 PB

ISBN 978-1-56145-331-3 HC
ISBN 978-1-56145-406-8 PB

ISBN 978-1-56145-358-0 HC
ISBN 978-1-56145-481-5 PB

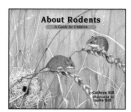

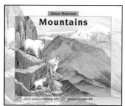

ISBN 978-1-56145-454-9 HC

ISBN 978-1-56145-488-4 HC

ISBN 978-1-56145-390-0 HC

ISBN 978-1-56145-432-7 HC

ISBN 978-1-56145-469-3 HC